OUR DAILY PRAYERS

OUR DAILY PRAYERS

*DEVOTIONS DRAWN
FROM THE HISTORIC BOOK OF COMMON PRAYER
AND OTHER TRADITIONAL ANGLICAN SOURCES*

Edited by the Rev'd John J. Lynch

All rights reserved. No part of this publication may be reproduced, stored in a retrieval system, or transmitted, in any form or by means, electronic, mechanical, photocopying or otherwise, without the prior permission of the author/editor.

© John J. Lynch, 2012

*Early in the morning do I cry unto thee; for in thy word is my trust.
Mine eyes prevent the night watches; that I might be occupied in thy word.
(Psalm 119:147-148)*

Introduction to Our Daily Prayers

Our Daily Prayers offers nothing that is especially new. Indeed the editor's goal has been to avoid novelty in all things apart from the presentation. He has sought rather to compile and arrange materials that are not readily available in a single, affordable and easily approachable format. He is aware that more recent devotional materials tend to be as bulky and complicated as the mediaeval service books that the Anglican Reformers insisted were too much for family use. It is hoped that this small book will provide a brief introduction to prayer in the Anglican tradition, not as textbook with lessons, but a friendly companion to the novice and experienced alike. The contents are taken from the historic editions of the Book of Common Prayer and from devotional materials published for private use across from the Reformation onwards. Some materials are commonly available; others have not been in print for many years. All are included for their usability and spiritual depth. May God bless all those who turn to him in prayer, especially the users of *Our Daily Prayers*.

A Note on the Structure of *Our Daily Prayers*

The structure of this volume is built around the order of the day, from morning to evening with topical prayers and devotions found between the two.

JJL

St. Simon and St. Jude, Apostles, 2012
Yorktown, Virginia

Contents

Preface	1
Morning Prayer for Families	5
A Shorter Form of Morning Prayer	7
Additional Morning Prayers	9
Canticles and Psalms	
Morning	11
Evening	12
For General Use	13
Prayers and Intercessions	15
For Family and Loves Ones	17
For the Church	18
Noonday	20
Thanksgivings	21
Collects for the Church Year	22
A Table of Psalms	25
Evening Prayer for Families	27
A Shorter Form of Evening Prayer	31
Additional Evening Prayers	33

Morning Prayer for Families
(BCP-USA 1789-1928)

The Master or Mistress having called together as many of the Family as can conveniently be present, let one of them, or any other who may be appointed, say as followeth, all kneeling, and repeating with him the Lord's Prayer.

OUR Father, who art in heaven, Hallowed be thy Name. Thy Kingdom come. Thy will be done, On earth as it is in heaven. Give us this day our daily bread. And forgive us our trespasses, As we forgive those who trespass against us. And lead us not into temptation, But deliver us from evil. For thine is the kingdom, and the power, and the glory, for ever and ever. Amen.

Here may follow the Collect for the day, or one of the Canticles.

Acknowledgment of God's Mercy and Preservation, especially through the Night past

ALMIGHTY and everlasting God, in whom we live and move and have our being; We, thy needy creatures, render thee our humble praises, for thy preservation of us from the beginning of our lives to this day, and especially for having delivered us from the dangers of the past night. For these thy mercies, we bless and magnify thy glorious Name; humbly beseeching thee to accept this our morning sacrifice of praise and thanksgiving; for his sake who lay down in the grave, and rose again for us, thy Son our Saviour Jesus Christ. *Amen.*

Dedication of Soul and Body to God's Service, with a Resolution to be growing daily in Goodness.

AND since it is of thy mercy, O gracious Father, that another day is added to our lives; We here dedicate both our souls and our bodies to thee and thy service, in a sober, righteous, and godly life: in which resolution, do thou, O merciful God, confirm and strengthen us; that, as we grow in age, we may grow in grace, and in the knowledge of our Lord and Saviour Jesus Christ. *Amen.*

Prayer for Grace to enable us to perform that Resolution.

BUT, O God, who knowest the weakness and corruption of our nature, and the manifold temptations which we daily meet with; We humbly beseech thee to have compassion on our infirmities, and to give us the constant assistance of thy Holy Spirit; that we may be effectually restrained from sin, and incited to our duty. Imprint upon our hearts such a dread of thy judgments, and such a grateful sense of thy goodness to us, as may make us both afraid and ashamed to offend thee. And, above all, keep in our minds a lively remembrance of that great day, in which we must give a strict account of our thoughts, words, and actions to him whom thou hast appointed the Judge of quick and dead, thy Son Jesus Christ our Lord. *Amen.*

*For Grace to guide and keep us the following Day,
and for God's Blessing on the business of the Same*

IN particular, we implore thy grace and protection for the ensuing day. Keep us temperate in all things, and diligent in our several callings. Grant us patience under our afflictions. Give us grace to be just and upright in all our dealings; quiet and peaceable; full of compassion; and ready to do good to all men, according to our abilities and opportunities. Direct us in all our ways. Defend us from all dangers and adversities; and be graciously pleased to take us, and all who are dear to us, under thy fatherly care and protection. These things, and whatever else thou shalt see to be necessary and convenient to us, we humbly beg, through the merits and mediation of thy Son Jesus Christ, our Lord and Saviour. *Amen.*

THE grace of our Lord Jesus Christ, and the love of God, and the fellowship of the Holy Ghost, be with us all evermore. *Amen.*

A Shorter Order of Morning Prayer for Families
(BCP-USA 1928)

After the reading of a brief portion of Holy Scripture, let the Head of the Household, or some other member of the family, say as followeth, all kneeling, and repeating with him the Lord's Prayer.

O send out thy light and thy truth, that they may lead me, and bring me unto thy holy hill, and to thy dwelling. *Psalm 43:3.*

Thus saith the high and lofty One that inhabiteth eternity, whose name is Holy; I dwell in the high and holy place, with him also that is of a contrite and humble spirit, to revive the spirit of the humble, and to revive the heart of the contrite ones. *Isaiah 57:15.*

The hour cometh, and now is, when the true worshippers shall worship the Father in spirit and in truth: for the Father seeketh such to worship him. *St. John 4:23.*

OUR Father, who art in heaven, Hallowed be thy Name. Thy kingdom come. Thy will be done, On earth as it is in heaven. Give us this day our daily bread. And forgive us our trespasses, As we forgive those who trespass against us. And lead us not into temptation, But deliver us from evil. For thine is the kingdom, and the power, and the glory, for ever and ever. Amen.

O LORD, our heavenly Father, Almighty and everlasting God, who hast safely brought us to the beginning of this day; Defend us in the same with thy mighty power; and grant that this day we fall into no sin, neither run into any kind of danger; but that all our doings, being ordered by thy governance, may be righteous in thy sight; through Jesus Christ our Lord. *Amen.*

Here may be added any special Prayers (or one of the Canticles).

THE grace of our Lord Jesus Christ, and the love of God, and the fellowship of the Holy Ghost, be with us all evermore. *Amen.*

Additional Morning Prayers

In the Morning
O GOD, the King eternal, who dividest the day from the darkness, and turnest the shadow of death into the morning; Drive far off from us all wrong desires, incline our hearts to keep thy law, and guide our feet into the way of peace; that having done thy will with cheerfulness while it was day, we may, when the night cometh, rejoice to give thee thanks; through Jesus Christ our Lord. *Amen.*

ALMIGHTY God, who alone gavest us the breath of life, and alone canst keep alive in us the holy desires thou dost impart; We beseech thee, for thy compassion's sake, to sanctify all our thoughts and endeavours; that we may neither begin an action without a pure intention nor continue it without thy blessing. And grant that, having the eyes of the mind opened to behold things invisible and unseen, we may in heart be inspired by thy wisdom, and in work be upheld by thy strength, and in the end be accepted of thee as thy faithful servants; through Jesus Christ our Saviour. *Amen.*   *(BCP 1928)*

A Collect for Peace
O GOD, who art the author of peace and lover of concord, in knowledge of whom standeth our eternal life, whose service is perfect freedom; Defend us thy humble servants in all assaults of our enemies; that we, surely trusting in thy defence, may not fear the power of any adversaries, through the might of Jesus Christ our Lord. *Amen.*   *(BCP 1549)*

For God's Blessing and Direction
PROCEEDING from glory to glory, we still glorify thee, O Father of Spirits, and pray thee for ever to continue thy goodness towards us. Direct our way aright, establish us in holy purposes, keep us unspotted in thy faith, let the enemy have no part in us, but conform us forever to the likeness of thy holy Son; lead us on to the perfect adoption of our souls, and to the redemption of our bodies from

corruption, and fill our hearts and tongues with everlasting praises of thy name; through Jesus Christ our Lord. *Amen.*   *(J. Taylor, 1658)*

A General Intercession.

O GOD, at whose word man goeth forth to his work and to his labour until the evening; Be merciful to all whose duties are difficult or burdensome, and comfort them concerning their toil. Shield from bodily accident and harm the workmen at their work. Protect the efforts of sober and honest industry, and suffer not the hire of the labourers to be kept back by fraud. Incline the heart of employers and of those whom they employ to mutual forbearance, fairness, and good-will. Give the spirit of governance and of a sound mind to all in places of authority. Bless all those who labour in works of mercy or in schools of good learning. Care for all aged persons, and all little children, the sick and the afflicted, and those who travel by land, air, or by sea. Remember all who by reason of weakness are overtasked, or because of poverty are forgotten. Let the sorrowful sighing of the prisoners come before thee; and according to the greatness of thy power, preserve thou those that are appointed to die. Give ear unto our prayer, O merciful and gracious Father, for the love of thy dear Son, our Saviour Jesus Christ. *Amen.*   *(BCP 1928)*

Canticles and Psalms
For Morning

Benedictus. (St. Luke 1:68-79.)

BLESSED be the Lord God of Israel; * for he hath visited and redeemed his people;

And hath raised up a mighty salvation for us, * in the house of his servant David;

As he spake by the mouth of his holy Prophets, * which have been since the world began;

That we should be saved from our enemies, * and from the hand of all that hate us.

To perform the mercy promised to our forefathers, * and to remember his holy covenant;

To perform the oath which he sware to our forefather Abraham, * that he would give us;

That we being delivered out of the hand of our enemies * might serve him without fear;

In holiness and righteousness before him, * all the days of our life.

And thou, child, shalt be called the prophet of the Highest: * for thou shalt go before the face of the Lord to prepare his ways;

To give knowledge of salvation unto his people * for the remission of their sins,

Through the tender mercy of our God; * whereby the day-spring from on high hath visited us;

To give light to them that sit in darkness, and in the shadow of death, * and to guide our feet into the way of peace.

Or

Jubilate Deo. (Psalm 100)

O BE joyful in the Lord, all ye lands: * serve the Lord with gladness, and come before his presence with a song.

Be ye sure that the Lord he is God; it is he that hath made us, and not we ourselves; * we are his people, and the sheep of his pasture.

O go your way into his gates with thanksgiving, and into his courts with praise; * be thankful unto him, and speak good of his Name.

For the Lord is gracious, his mercy is everlasting; * and his truth endureth from generation to generation.

<u>*For Evening*</u>

Magnificat. (St. Luke 1:46-55.)
MY soul doth magnify the Lord, * and my spirit hath rejoiced in God my Saviour.

For he hath regarded * the lowliness of his handmaiden.

For behold, from henceforth * all generations shall call me blessed.

For he that is mighty hath magnified me; * and holy is his Name.

And his mercy is on them that fear him * throughout all generations.

He hath showed strength with his arm; * he hath scattered the proud in the imagination of their hearts.

He hath put down the mighty from their seat, * and hath exalted the humble and meek.

He hath filled the hungry with good things; * and the rich he hath sent empty away.

He remembering his mercy hath holpen his servant Israel; * as he promised to our forefathers, Abraham and his seed, for ever.

Or

Nunc dimittis. (St. Luke 2:29-32.)
LORD, now lettest thou thy servant depart in peace, * according to thy word.

For mine eyes have seen * thy salvation,

Which thou hast prepared * before the face of all people;

To be a light to lighten the Gentiles, * and to be the glory of thy people Israel.

General Canticles

Gloria in excelsis

GLORY be to God on high, and on earth peace, good will towards men. We praise thee, we bless thee, we worship thee, we glorify thee, we give thanks to thee for thy great glory, O Lord God, heavenly King, God the Father Almighty.

O Lord, the only-begotten Son, Jesus Christ; O Lord God, Lamb of God, Son of the Father, that takest away the sins of the world, have mercy upon us. Thou that takest away the sins of the world, receive our prayer. Thou that sittest at the right hand of God the Father, have mercy upon us.

Gloria Patri

GLORY be to the Father, and to the Son, and the Holy Ghost,*
As it was in the beginning, is now, and ever shall be, world without end.

Salvator Mundi

O Saviour of the World, by thy Cross and precious Blood, thou hast redeemed world: Save and help us, we humbly beseech thee, O Lord.

Veni Creator Spiritus

Come, Holy Ghost, our souls inspire
And lighten with celestial fire.
Thou the anointing Spirit, art,
Who dost thy sevenfold gifts impart.
Thy blessed unction from above,
Is comfort, life, and fire of love:
Enable with perpetual light,
The dullness of our blinded sight:
Anoint and cheer our soiled face,
With the abundance of thy grace:
Keep far our foes; give peace at home;
Where thou art guide, no ill can come.
Teach us to Know the Father, Son,
And thee, of both to be but One;
That through the ages all along,

This may be our endless song;
Praise to thy Eternal Merit,
Father, Son, and Holy Spirit. *Amen.*   *(Latin, BCP 1662)*

The Apostles Creed

I BELIEVE in God the Father Almighty, Maker of heaven and earth: And in Jesus Christ his only Son our Lord: Who was conceived by the Holy Ghost, Born of the Virgin Mary: Suffered under Pontius Pilate, Was crucified, dead, and buried: He descended into hell; The third day he rose again from the dead: He ascended into heaven, And sitteth on the right hand of God the Father Almighty: From thence he shall come to judge the quick and the dead. I believe in the Holy Ghost: The holy Catholic Church; The Communion of Saints: The Forgiveness of sins: The Resurrection of the body: And the Life everlasting. *Amen.*

Prayers and Intercessions

For the Spirit of Prayer
O Almighty God, who hast bidden us seek that we may find, and who pourest out on all who desire it, the spirit of grace and of supplication; Deliver us, when we draw nigh to thee, from coldness of heart and wandering of mind, that with steadfast thoughts and kindled affections we may worship thee in spirit and in truth; through Jesus Christ our Lord. *Amen.* *(BCP 1928)*

A Prayer of Saint Richard of Chichester.
O HOLY JESUS, Most merciful Redeemer, Friend and Brother, may I know thee more clearly, love thee more dearly, and follow thee more nearly. *Amen.*

The General Confession
ALMIGHTY and most merciful Father; We have erred, and strayed from thy ways like lost sheep. We have followed too much the devices and desires of our own hearts. We have offended against thy holy laws. We have left undone those things which we ought to have done; And we have done those things which we ought not to have done; And there is no health in us. But thou, O Lord, have mercy upon us, miserable offenders. Spare thou those, O God, who confess their faults. Restore thou those who are penitent; According to thy promises declared unto mankind In Christ Jesus our Lord. And grant, O most merciful Father, for his sake; That we may hereafter live a godly, righteous, and sober life, To the glory of thy holy Name. *Amen.* *(BCP 1549)*

Another Confession of Sin
We have sinned, Lord, we have sinned grievously, we have done unjustly, we have lived wickedly : we are sorry, therefore, Lord, yea, we most sorry, that we are no more sorry for our sins : but thou. Lord God, Father of all mercies, we humbly beseech thee, be not angry with us forever for our great and manifold sins, neither deal with us according to our deserts, neither reward us according to our

wickedness ; but even for thy self, Lord God, and for thy holy name's sake, for thy most gracious assured promises made unto penitent sinners in tliy holy word, the word of truth, for thy infinite mercies which are in thy dearly beloved Son Jesus Christ our Saviour, for his sake, for his death and precious blood, be merciful unto us sinners ; and so we, who have most grievously offended thy divine majesty, shall continually magnify thy great and infinite mercy, through our Saviour Jesus Christ, to whom with thee and the Holy Ghost be all honour and glory, world without end. *Amen.*
(A Form of Prayer to be Used, 1572)

A Prayer of Praise and Trust

O ALMIGHTY GOD, I bless and praise thee for all thy goodness and loving-kindness. I believe Thou art a God of perfect love. I believe thou art my Heavenly Father, watching over me and all I love in this world and beyond. I believe that Jesus Christ thy only Son died for me and loves me still, and is near me at all times to help and strengthen me. I believe thy Holy Spirit ever pleads in my heart, and every thought of holiness is his alone. I believe that all my sorrows have a place in thy mind, and that thou art filled with loving compassion for all suffering and pain. I believe thou lovest all men, and carest for all those I love, and so I would leave them in thy care. I believe thou forgivest all sins of those who in loving repentance come to thee. O Loving God, I desire to love thee more. I praise thy Holy Name. Help me to reverence and adore thee more deeply. Give me the power to love thee more truly; for Jesus' sake. *Amen.*
(The Melanesian Book of Common Prayer, 1938)

Acts of Faith, Hope, and Love

I believe in thee, O God, Father, Son, and Holy Ghost, my Creator, and my Redeemer, and my Sanctifier; I believe that thou art All-Holy, Just and Merciful. I believe that thou art willing to pardon and to save me, if I repent and forsake my sins. O my God, strengthen and increase my faith, and grant me the grace of a true repentance, for Jesus Christ's sake. *Amen.*

I hope in thee, O my God, because thou art Almighty, Faithful, and Long-suffering. I humbly trust that thou wilt pardon my sins for the sake of thy dear Son Jesus Christ, who suffered and died for me upon the Cross; and that thou wilt cleanse my sinful soul in his Precious Blood, and make me holy, and bring me safe to everlasting life. O Lord, in thee have I trusted, let me never be confounded. *Amen.*

I love thee, O my God, above all things, because thou hast been so good, so patient, so loving to me, notwithstanding all the sins by which I have so grievously offended Thee. I love thee, O Blessed Jesus, my Saviour, because thou didst suffer so much for love of me, an ungrateful sinner, and didst die on the Cross for my salvation. O make me love thee more and more, and show my love to thee by faithfully keeping thy Commandments all the days of my life. *Amen.*
(Book of Offices, 1914)

Prayers for Family and Loved Ones

For Those We Love
ALMIGHTY God, we entrust all who are dear to us to thy never-failing care and love, for this life and the life to come; knowing that thou art doing for them better things than we can desire or pray for; through Jesus Christ our Lord. *Amen.* *(BCP 1928)*

For Children
ALMIGHTY God, heavenly Father, who hast blessed us with the joy and care of children; Give us light and strength so to train them, that they may love whatsoever things are true and pure and lovely and of good report, following the example of their Saviour Jesus Christ. *Amen.* *(BCP 1928)*

O LORD Jesus Christ, who dost embrace children with the arms of thy mercy, and dost make them living members of thy Church; Give them grace, we pray thee, to stand fast in thy faith, to obey thy word, and to abide in thy love; that, being made strong by thy Holy Spirit, they may resist temptation and overcome evil, and may rejoice in the

life that now is, and dwell with thee in the life that is to come; through thy merits, O merciful Saviour, who with the Father and the Holy Ghost livest and reignest one God, world without end. *Amen.*
(BCP 1928)

For a Blessing on the Families of the Land
ALMIGHTY God, our heavenly Father, who settest the solitary in families; We commend to thy continual care the homes in which thy people dwell. Put far from them, we beseech thee, every root of bitterness, the desire of vain-glory, and the pride of life. Fill them with faith, virtue, knowledge, temperance, patience, godliness. Knit together in constant affection those who, in holy wedlock, have been made one flesh; turn the heart of the fathers to the children, and the heart of the children to the fathers; and so enkindle fervent charity among us all, that we be evermore kindly affectioned with brotherly love; through Jesus Christ our Lord. *Amen.*   *(BCP 1928)*

For those who have none to pray for them
O Lord Jesus Christ, who ever livest to make intercession for us, let Thy mercy be extended to all those who have none upon earth to pray for them in thy Name, and bring them, for thine own sake, to a participation of thy grace on earth, that they may praise thee with all thy saints in thine everlasting glory. *Amen.*   *(BO 1914)*

Prayers for the Church

For the Purification of the Church From Error
O Eternal God and merciful Father, we humbly pray for thy holy Church throughout the world, that it being purged from false philosophy and vain deceit, we may live and act as befits the members of the mystical Body of thy Son, and in the end be found acceptable unto thee; through the same Jesus Christ our Lord. *Amen.*
(BO 1914)

An Intercession for the Church
We beseech thee, O Lord, let the strong crying of thy Church ever be acceptable unto thee; that receiving forgiveness of sins, it may

become devout by the working of thy grace, and tranquil under the protection of thy power; through Jesus Christ our Lord. *Amen.*

(BO 1914)

For the Parish

ALMIGHTY God, we beseech thee to bless this our parish. Forgive us our many and grievous sins. Draw us nearer to thyself, and cause true religion to increase and abound amongst us. Prosper the reading and preaching of thy Word, and bless all the ministrations of thy Church. Give patience to the sick and afflicted, and make their sufferings a blessing to them. Visit with thy favour the schools and all who teach or learn therein; and make us to grow in grace and in the knowledge of thee and of thy dear Son, whom to know is life eternal. Hear us for the sake of him who died for us, Jesus Christ our Lord. *Amen.* *(Irish BCP 1926)*

For the Bishop of the Diocese

O God, the Pastor and Ruler of thy faithful servants, look down in mercy on thy servant, N. our bishop. Do thou evermore guide, defend, comfort, sanctify and save him, and grant him by thy grace so to advance in word and good example, that he may, with the flock committed to him, attain to everlasting life; through Jesus Christ our Lord. *Amen.* *(BO 1914)*

For Charity amongst Christians

O Lord Jesus Christ, who hast commanded us to love one another; put an end to the unhappy divisions of those who are called by thy name. Come quickly and bind us together in the full revelation of thy love, and let the desire for thine appearing unite us even now while we wait for thee. Teach us to realize that the ordinances of thy grace bind us to each other as well as unto thee; and let us not so misuse the means of our salvation as to foster a spirit of division by what should be the channels of thy love. Enable us to love one another in thee and for thee, until all our imperfections are done away, and we shall shine forth in thy light, and rejoice in the manifestations of thy love. In thy Love let us triumph over all difference of condition, all the estrangements of race, all the prejudices of education, all the pride of self-will. In thy love let us be humble; in thy love let us be one; that in thy love we may be exalted, and in thy love we may be thine for ever. *Amen.* *(BO 1914)*

For Noonday

At Midday

Blessed Saviour, who at this hour didst hang upon the Cross, stretching forth Thy loving arms; Grant that all mankind may look unto Thee and be saved, through Thy mercies and merits who livest and reignest with the Father and the Holy Ghost, ever one God, world without end. *Amen.* *(BO 1914)*

The Angelus

THE ANGEL of the Lord declared unto Mary,
And she conceived by the Holy Ghost.
Hail, Mary, full of grace, the Lord is with thee; blessed art thou amongst women, and blessed is the fruit of thy womb, Jesus.
Holy Mary, Mother of God, pray for us sinners, now and at the hour of our death. Amen.

Behold the handmaid of the Lord;
Be it unto the according to Thy Word.
Hail, Mary . . .

And the Word was made Flesh,
And dwelt among us.
Hail, Mary . . .
Pray for us, O holy Mother of God;
That we may be made worthy of the promises of Christ.

Let us pray.

WE beseech thee, O Lord, to pour thy grace into our hearts; that as we have known the Incarnation of thy Son Jesus Christ by the message of an Angel, so by his Cross and Passion we may be brought unto the glory of his Resurrection; through the same Jesus Christ our Lord. *Amen.* *(Melanesian BCP 1938)*

Thanksgivings

A Daily Thanksgiving

O LOVING GOD, I thank thee for thy care of me throughout my life. (For the blessing of my birth in a Christian home.)
(For my Baptism) (and Confirmation.)
(For every Communion.)
For every sin forgiven.
For each new beginning allowed by thy love.
For my home.
For the love of every dear friend.
For the kindness that I never can repay.
For those whose love has drawn me near to thee.
For all who have helped me in my spiritual life.
For all who have cared for my bodily needs.
For times of pleasure and happiness.
For trials or illnesses permitted that I might be drawn nearer to thee.
For the love of Jesus my Lord.
For the glory of his friendship.
For the Holy Spirit's guidance.
For all answers to my prayers.
For the overshadowing of thine Eternal Presence.
O Lord, I thank thee, I praise thee, I bless thee. O make me worthier of thy love; help me to consecrate my life to thee afresh in gratitude and love of thy dear Son. *Amen.*   *(Melanesian BCP 1938)*

A General Thanksgiving

ALMIGHTY God, Father of all mercies, we, thine unworthy servants, do give thee most humble and hearty thanks for all thy goodness and loving-kindness to us, and to all men; [* *particularly to those who desire now to offer up their praises and thanksgivings for thy late mercies vouchsafed unto them.*] We bless thee for our creation, preservation, and all the blessings of this life; but above all, for thine inestimable love in the redemption of the world by our Lord Jesus Christ; for the means of grace, and for the hope of glory. And, we beseech thee, give us that due sense of all thy mercies, that our hearts may be unfeignedly thankful; and that we show forth thy praise, not only with our lips, but in our lives, by giving up our selves to thy service, and by walking before thee in holiness and righteousness all our days; through Jesus Christ our Lord, to whom, with thee and the Holy Ghost, be all honour and glory, world without end. *Amen.*

(BCP 1662)

Collects for Church Year

Advent

ALMIGHTY God, give us grace that we may cast away the works of darkness, and put upon us the armour of light, now in the time of this mortal life, in which thy Son Jesus Christ came to visit us in great humility; that in the last day, when he shall come again in his glorious majesty to judge both the quick and the dead, we may rise to the life immortal, through him who liveth and reigneth with thee and the Holy Ghost, now and ever. *Amen.*

Christmas

ALMIGHTY God, who hast given us thy only-begotten Son to take our nature upon him, and as at this time to be born of a pure virgin; Grant that we being regenerate, and made thy children by adoption and grace, may daily be renewed by thy Holy Spirit; through the same our Lord Jesus Christ, who liveth and reigneth with thee and the same Spirit ever, one God, world without end. *Amen.*

Epiphany

O GOD, who by the leading of a star didst manifest thy only-begotten Son to the Gentiles; Mercifully grant that we, who know thee now by faith, may after this life have the fruition of thy glorious Godhead; through the same thy Son Jesus Christ our Lord. *Amen.*

Ash Wednesday and Lent

ALMIGHTY and everlasting God, who hatest nothing that thou hast made, and dost forgive the sins of all those who are penitent; Create and make in us new and contrite hearts, that we, worthily lamenting our sins and acknowledging our wretchedness, may obtain of thee, the God of all mercy, perfect remission and forgiveness; through Jesus Christ our Lord. *Amen.*

Passiontide

ALMIGHTY and everlasting God, who, of thy tender love towards mankind, hast sent thy Son, our Saviour Jesus Christ, to take upon him our flesh, and to suffer death upon the cross, that all mankind should follow the example of his great humility; Mercifully grant, that we may both follow the example of his patience, and also be made partakers of his resurrection; through the same Jesus Christ our Lord. *Amen.*

Easter

ALMIGHTY God, who through thine only-begotten Son Jesus Christ hast overcome death, and opened unto us the gate of everlasting life; We humbly beseech thee that, as by thy special grace preventing us thou dost put into our minds good desires, so by thy continual help we may bring the same to good effect; through the same Jesus Christ our Lord, who liveth and reigneth with thee and the Holy Ghost ever, one God, world without end. *Amen.*

Ascension

GRANT, we beseech thee, Almighty God, that like as we do believe thy only-begotten Son our Lord Jesus Christ to have ascended into the heavens; so we may also in heart and mind thither ascend, and with him continually dwell, who liveth and reigneth with thee and the Holy Ghost, one God, world without end. *Amen.*

Pentecost

O GOD, who as at this time didst teach the hearts of thy faithful people, by sending to them the light of thy Holy Spirit; Grant us by the same Spirit to have a right judgment in all things, and evermore to rejoice in his holy comfort; through the merits of Christ Jesus our Saviour, who liveth and reigneth with thee, in the unity of the same Spirit, one God, world without end. *Amen.*

Trinity

ALMIGHTY and everlasting God, who hast given unto us thy servants grace, by the confession of a true faith to acknowledge the glory of the eternal Trinity, and in the power of thy Divine Majesty to worship the Unity; We beseech thee, that thou wouldst keep us steadfast in this faith, and evermore defend us from all adversities, who livest and reignest, one God, world without end. *Amen.*

All Saints

O ALMIGHTY God, who hast knit together thine elect in one communion and fellowship, in the mystical body of thy Son Christ our Lord; Grant us grace so to follow thy blessed Saints in all virtuous and godly living, that we may come to those unspeakable joys which thou hast prepared for those who unfeignedly love thee; through the same thy Son Jesus Christ our Lord. *Amen.*

The Blessed Virgin Mary

O Merciful Father, hear the prayers of thy servants who commemorate the *Feast* of the Mother of the Lord; and grant that by the incarnation of thy dear Son we may indeed be made nigh unto him, who liveth and reigneth with thee and the Holy Ghost; one God, world without end. *Amen.* *(Proposed BCP 1928)*

A Table of Psalms

The reading of the Psalms is very proper for exciting oneself to piety and devotion, and in the table below the faithful will find the most apt psalm according to their particular needs.

The Greatness of God, in himself and his creatures. —8, 19, 104, 139, 145.
To contemplate and praise God's grandeur. —18, 97, 107, 135, 147.
An invitation to praise God. —95, 96, 108, 113, 148.
Prophecies of Jesus Christ's Birth, Death, and Resurrection. —16, 22, 40, 85, 96.
The Kingdom of God, the joy of Saints; the Ascension. —24, 47, 68, 97, 99, 110.
The Kingdom of Christ, exhortation to rulers and judges. —2, 58, 82, 101, 138.
The Second Coming of Christ. —50, 97, 99, 149.
The Spread of the Church; conversion of the nations; wonderful effects of God's Word. —29, 45, 72, 76, 87, 111.
To pray for the Church, especially during affliction. —10, 44, 46, 74, 79, 80.
God's protection of the righteous. —11, 23, 27, 121, 125, 127.
Unhappiness of those who love material things. —49, 52, 115, 140.
Happiness of the righteous and wretchedness of the wicked. —1, 15, 32, 69, 126, 128.
Fear of God's judgments. —7, 21, 36, 50, 64, 75.
For the conversion of the heart —5, 25, 30, 39.
Addressing the heart of God. —42, 61, 63, 73, 84, 122.
To despise earthly goods. —43, 120, 137, 142.
The desire of eternal glory. —15, 42, 84, 122.
For the forgiveness of sins. —6, 32, 38, 51, 102, 130, 143.
Hope in God. —73, 62, 71, 90, 112, 123.
To accept God's will. —39, 55, 131, 143.
For trust in God's goodness. —3, 4, 57, 60, 91, 124.
For the spirit of prayer. —17, 86, 90, 141.
For God's help during periods of trouble. —26, 31, 54, 69, 70, 129.
Against the evil of persecutors. —12, 14, 28, 35, 59, 83.
To turn to God in affliction and sadness. —6, 13, 41, 77, 88, 129.
Thanksgiving. —30, 34, 66, 81, 100, 103, 116, 118, 136, 144.

(Liturgy of the Spanish Reformed Episcopal Church, 1954)

Evening Prayer for Families
(BCP USA 1789-1928)

The Family being together, a little before bedtime, let the Master or Mistress, or any other who may be appointed, say as followeth, all kneeling, and repeating with him the Lord's Prayer.

OUR Father, who art in heaven, Hallowed be thy Name. Thy kingdom come. Thy will be done, On earth as it is in heaven. Give us this day our daily bread. And forgive us our trespasses, As we forgive those who trespass against us. And lead us not into temptation, But deliver us from evil. For thine is the kingdom, and the power, and the glory, for ever and ever. *Amen.*

Here may follow the Collect for the day (or one of the Canticles).

Confession of Sins, with a Prayer for Contrition and Pardon

MOST merciful God, who art of purer eyes than to behold iniquity, and hast promised forgiveness to all those who confess and forsake their sins; We come before thee in an humble sense of our own unworthiness, acknowledging our manifold transgressions of thy righteous laws.* But, O gracious Father, who desirest not the death of a sinner, look upon us, we beseech thee, in mercy, and forgive us all our transgressions. Make us deeply sensible of the great evil of them; and work in us a hearty contrition; that we may obtain forgiveness at thy hands, who art ever ready to receive humble and penitent sinners; for the sake of thy Son Jesus Christ, our only Saviour and Redeemer. *Amen.*

Prayer for Grace to reform and grow Better

AND lest, through our own frailty, or the temptations which encompass us, we be drawn again into sin, vouchsafe us, we beseech thee, the direction and assistance of thy Holy Spirit. Reform whatever is amiss in the temper and disposition of our souls; that no unclean thoughts, unlawful designs, or inordinate desires, may rest there. Purge our hearts from envy, hatred, and malice; that we may never suffer the sun to go down upon our wrath; but may always go to our rest in peace, charity, and good-will, with a conscience void of offence towards thee, and towards men; that so we may be preserved pure and blameless, unto the coming of our Lord and Saviour Jesus Christ. *Amen.*

The Intercession

AND accept, O Lord, our intercessions for all mankind. Let the light of thy Gospel shine upon all nations; and may as many as have received it, live as becomes it. Be gracious unto thy Church; and grant that every member of the same, in his vocation and ministry, may serve thee faithfully. Bless all in authority over us; and so rule their hearts and strengthen their hands, that they may punish wickedness and vice, and maintain thy true religion and virtue. Send down thy blessings, temporal and spiritual, upon all our relations, friends, and neighbours. Reward all who have done us good, and pardon all those who have done or wish us evil, and give them repentance and better minds. Be merciful to all who are in any trouble; and do thou, the God of pity, administer to them according to their several necessities; for his sake who went about doing good, thy Son our Saviour Jesus Christ. *Amen.*

The Thanksgiving

TO our prayers, O Lord, we join our unfeigned thanks for all thy mercies; for our being, our reason, and all other endowments and faculties of soul and body; for our health, friends, food, and raiment, and all the other comforts and conveniences of life. Above all, we adore thy mercy in sending thy only Son into the world, to redeem us from sin and eternal death, and in giving us the knowledge and sense of our duty towards thee. We bless thee for thy patience with us, notwithstanding our many and great provocations; for all the directions, assistances, and comforts of thy Holy Spirit; for thy continual care and watchful providence over us through the whole course of our lives; and particularly for the mercies and benefits of the past day; beseeching thee to continue these thy blessings to us, and to give us grace to show our thankfulness in a sincere obedience to his laws, through whose merits and intercession we received them all, thy Son our Saviour Jesus Christ. *Amen.*

Prayer for God's Protection through the Night following.
IN particular, we beseech thee to continue thy gracious protection to us this night. Defend us from all dangers and mischiefs, and from the fear of them; that we may enjoy such refreshing sleep as may fit us for the duties of the coming day. And grant us grace always to live in such a state that we may never be afraid to die; so that, living and dying, we may be thine, through the merits and satisfaction of thy Son Christ Jesus, in whose Name we offer up these our imperfect prayers. *Amen.*

THE grace of our Lord Jesus Christ, and the love of God, and the fellowship of the Holy Ghost, be with us all evermore. *Amen.*

On Sundays, and on other days when it may be convenient, it will be proper to begin with a Chapter, or part of a Chapter, from the New Testament.

A Shorter Order of Evening Prayer for Families
(BCP-USA 1928)

After the reading of a brief portion of Holy Scripture, let the Head of the Household, or some other member of the family, say as followeth, all kneeling and repeating with him the Lord's Prayer.

Let my prayer be set forth in thy sight as the incense; and let the lifting up of my hands be an evening sacrifice. *Psalm 14:2.*

O worship the Lord in the beauty of holiness; let the whole earth stand in awe of him. *Psalm 96:9.*

Let the words of my mouth, and the meditation of my heart, be always acceptable in thy sight, O Lord, my strength and my redeemer. *Psalm 19:14.*

OUR Father, who art in heaven, Hallowed be thy Name. Thy kingdom come. Thy will be done, On earth as it is in heaven. Give us this day our daily bread. And forgive us our trespasses, As we forgive those who trespass against us. And lead us not into temptation, But deliver us from evil. For thine is the kingdom, and the power, and the glory, for ever and ever. Amen.

LIGHTEN our darkness, we beseech thee, O Lord; and by thy great mercy defend us from all perils and dangers of this night; for the love of thy only Son, our Saviour, Jesus Christ. *Amen.*

Here may be added any special Prayers (or one of the Canticles).

THE Lord bless us and keep us. The Lord make his face to shine upon us, and be gracious unto us. The Lord lift up his countenance upon us, and give us peace, this night and evermore. *Amen.*

Additional Evening Prayers

At Night

O LORD, support us all the day long, until the shadows lengthen and the evening comes, and the busy world is hushed, and the fever of life is over, and our work is done. Then in thy mercy grant us a safe lodging, and a holy rest, and peace at the last. *Amen.*

O GOD, who art the life of mortal men, the light of the faithful, the strength of those who labour, and the repose of the dead; We thank thee for the timely blessings of the day, and humbly supplicate thy merciful protection all this night. Bring us, we beseech thee, in safety to the morning hours; through him who died for us and rose again, thy Son, our Saviour Jesus Christ. *Amen.*   *(BCP 1928)*

A Collect for Peace

O GOD, from whom all holy desires, all good counsels, and all just works do proceed; Give unto thy servants that peace which the world cannot give; that our hearts may be set to obey thy commandments, and also that by thee, we, being defended from the fear of our enemies, may pass our time in rest and quietness; through the merits of Jesus Christ our Saviour. *Amen.*   *(BCP 1549)*

A Prayer for the Evening

Eternal God, Almighty Father of Men and Angels, by whose care and providence I am preserved and blessed, comforted and assisted, I humbly beg of thee to pardon the sins and follies of this day, the weaknesses of my services, and the strength of my passions, the rashness of my words, and the vanity and evil of my actions. O just and dear God, how long shall I confess my sins, and pray against them, and yet fall under them! O let it be so no more, let me never return to the follies of which I am ashamed, which bring sorrow, and death, and thy displeasure, worse than death. Give me a command over my evil inclinations, and a perfect hatred of sin, and a love to thee above all the desires of this world. Be pleased to bless and preserve me this night from all sin, and all violence of Chance, and the malice of the Spirits of darkness: watch over me in my sleep, and whether sleep or wake, let me be thy servant. Be thou first and last in all my thoughts, and the guide and continual assistance of all my actions: Preserve my body, pardon the sin of my soul, and sanctify my soul; let me always live holily, and justly, and soberly; and when I die, receive my soul into thy hands, O holy and ever Blessed Jesus, that I may lie in thy bosom, and long for thy coming, and hear thy blessed Sentence at Doomsday, and behold thy face, and live in thy Kingdome, singing praises to God for ever and ever. *Amen.*

(J. Taylor 1655)

Made in the USA
Monee, IL
17 July 2022